Pupil's Book

Elizabeth Gray - Virginia Evans

Express Publishing

Follow me!

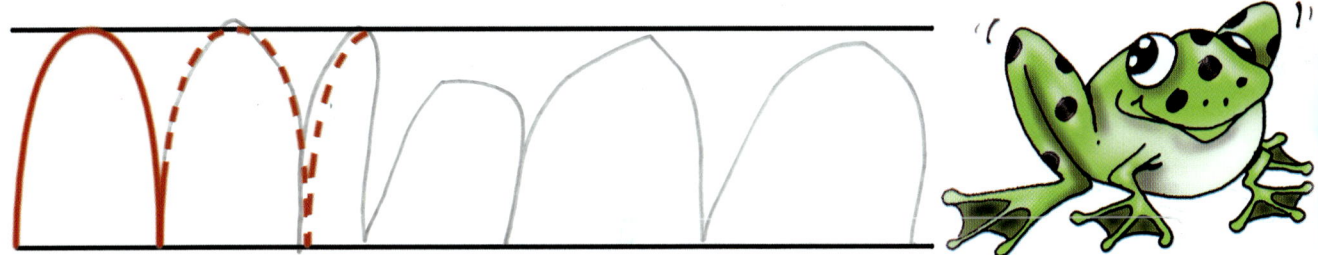
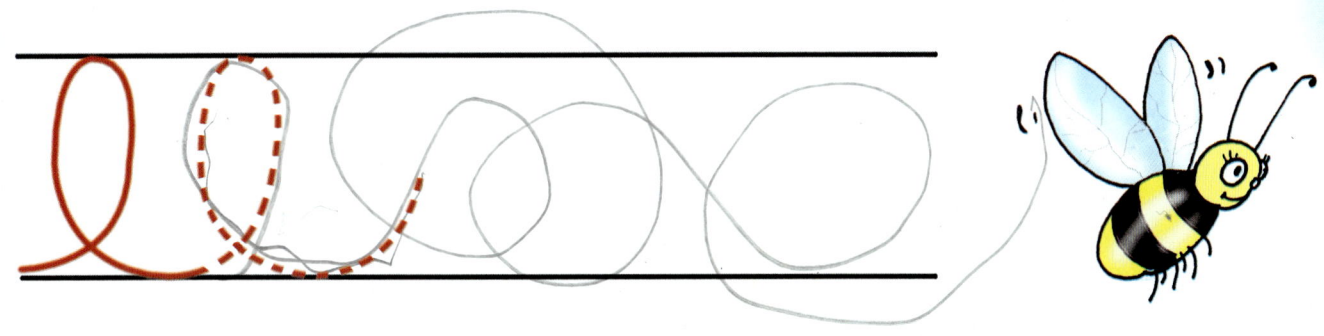
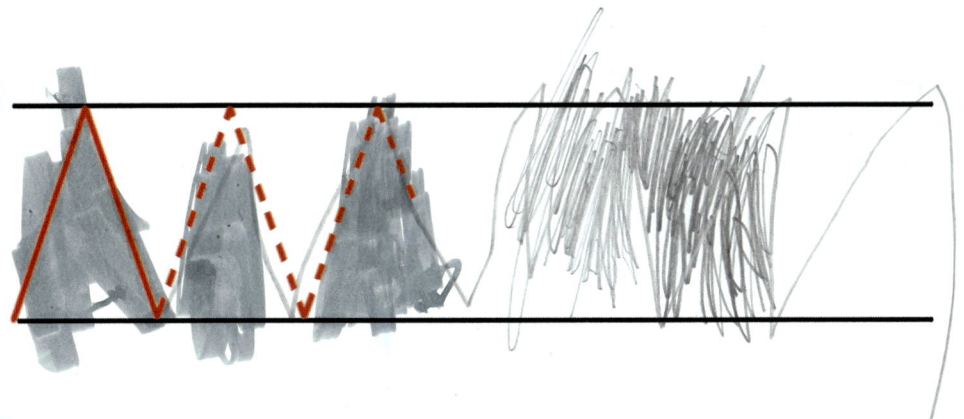

Follow me!

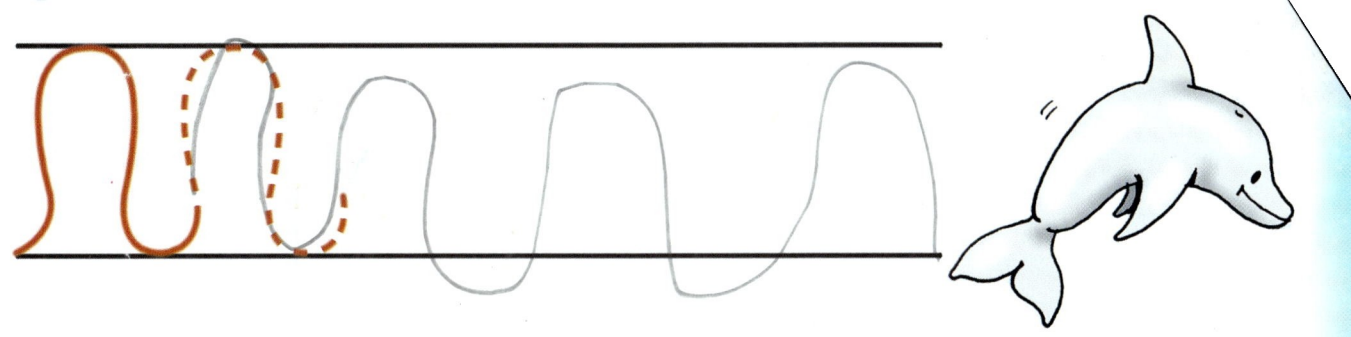
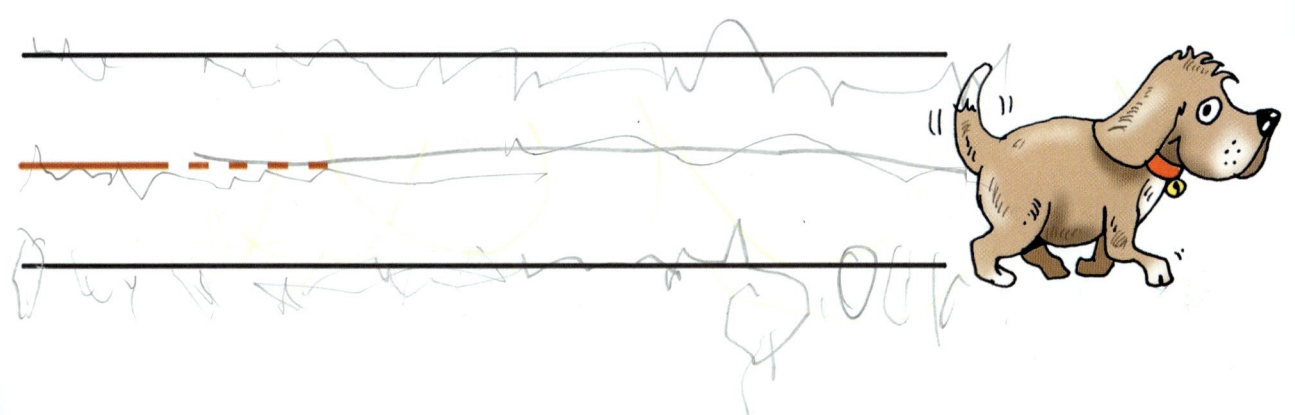
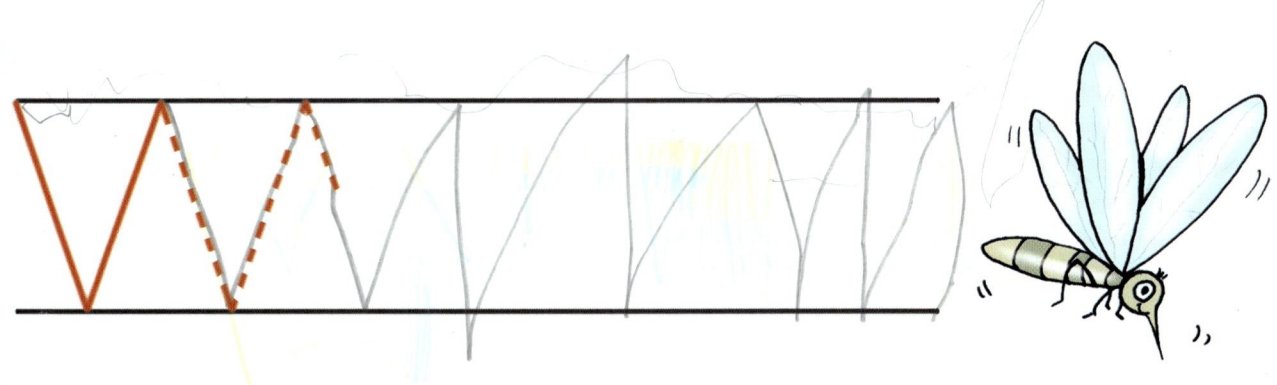

My letters!

a   ant
c   cat
e   egg
g   glass

b   bed
d   dog
f   flag
h   horse

My letters!

My letters!

i  ink

j  jug

k  kangaroo

l  lamp

m  mouse

n  nest

o  orange

p  pin

q  queen

My letters!

r rabbit
s snake
t tree
u umbrella
v vest
w window
x box
y yacht
z zip

cat, dog

red
blue
green
yellow

Hey, diddle, diddle,

The c _ _ and the fiddle,

The cow jumped over the moon.

The little d _ _ laughed

To see such fun,

And the dish ran away with the spoon!

hen, egg, hat

h  — hhh

e — eee

n — nnn

hen

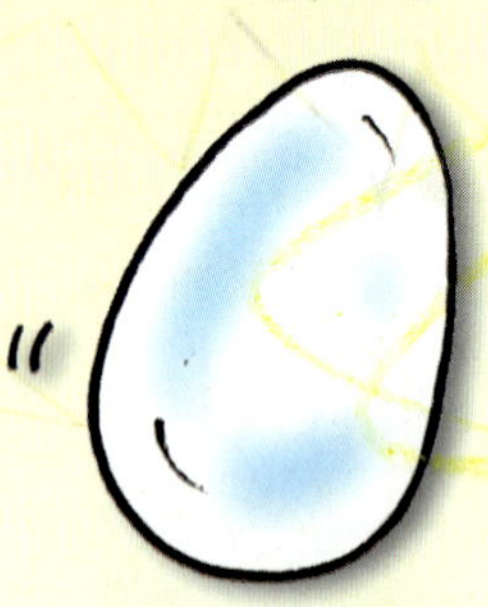

egg

hat

hen, egg, hat

cathathenegg

Higglety, pigglety,

My red h——,

She lays e——s,

For gentlemen!

Sometimes nine,

And sometimes ten,

Higglety, pigglety,

My red hen!

bell, well, vest

bell, well, vest

bell   vest

Ring the b _ _ _ ,

Ding - a - ling - a - ling!

On the w _ _ _ ,

Ding - a - ling - a - ling!

Ring it loud,

Ring it clear,

Ring for everyone to hear!

fox, box, zip

A-hunting we will go!

A-hunting we will go!

To catch a _ _ _

And put it in a _ _ _

And never let it go!

jug, mug, jam

jug

mug

jam

jug, mug, jam

☑ tree ☐ egg ☐ jug
☐ hen   ☑ vest ☑ jam

☐ glass ☑ bed ☑ zip
☑ mug   ☐ dog ☐ pin

Jack and Jill went up the hill

To fetch a ____ 🫖 of water.

Jack fell down and broke his crown

And Jill came tumbling after!

yoyo, pony, star

Yankee-Doodle went to town,

Riding on a _____.

He put a feather in his cap

And called it macaroni!

queen, king

qu qu

k k k

queen

king

queen, king

p o n y

k _ _ _ _

q _ _ _ _ _

"Hello, how are you?"

Said the queen of Hearts.

"I'm fine, I'm fine!" said Jack.

"Let's sing! Let's sing!"

Said the queen to the king

And then Jack said "Good luck!"

My numbers!

1 one
2 two
3 three
4 four
5 five
6 six
7 seven
8 eight
9 nine
10 ten

3 three

☐ ....

☐ ....

☐ ....

☐ ....

☐ ....

28

My numbers!

three	🐟🐟🐟🐟🐟🐟🐟🐟🐟🐟
six	⭐⭐⭐⭐⭐⭐⭐⭐⭐⭐
eight	🥚🥚🥚🥚🥚🥚🥚🥚🥚🥚
two	🪀🪀🪀🪀🪀🪀🪀🪀🪀🪀

One, two, three, four, _ _ _ _ ,

"Once I caught a fish alive!

Six, seven, eight, nine, _ _ _ ,

Then I let it go again!

Why did you let it go?

Because it bit my finger so!

Which finger did it bite?

This little finger on my right!

sheep, fish, ship

sh

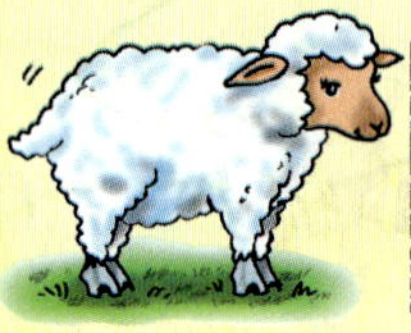

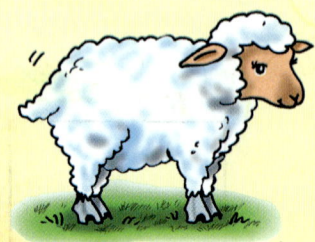

sh sh

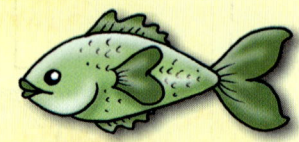

sheep

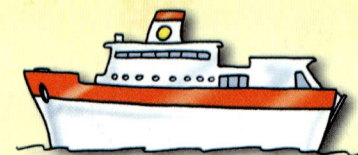

fish

ship

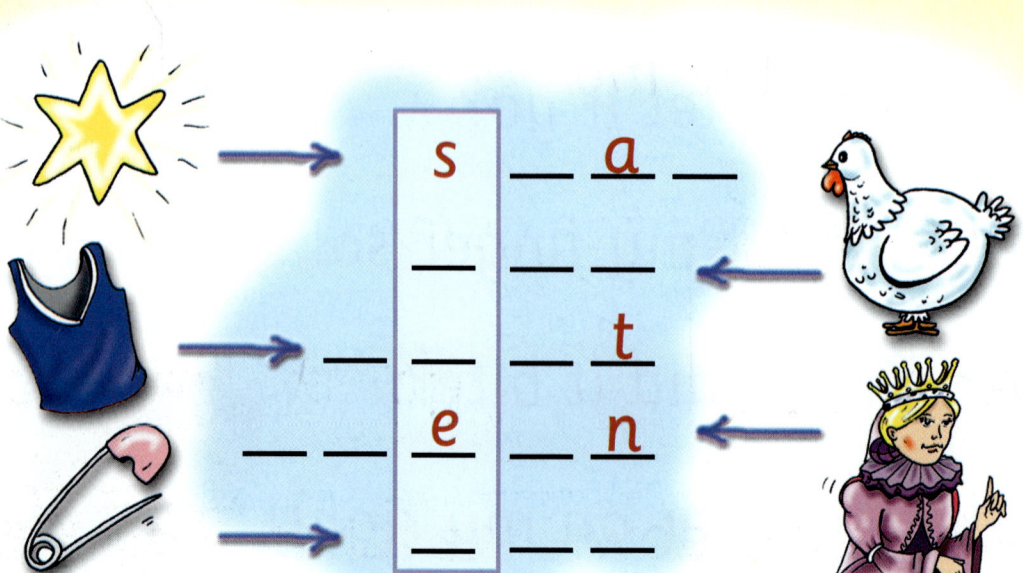

How many?

sheep, fish, ship

Baa, baa, black sheep,

Have you any wool?

Yes, sir! Yes, sir!

Three bags full!

One for the master

And one for the dame

And one  for the little boy

Who lives down the lane!

chick, cheese

ch

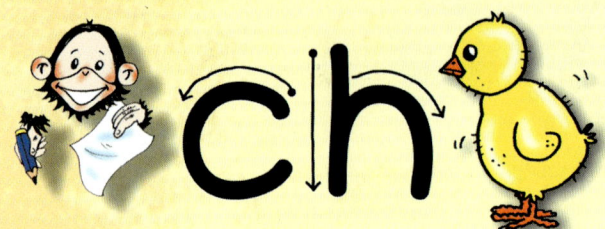

ch ch

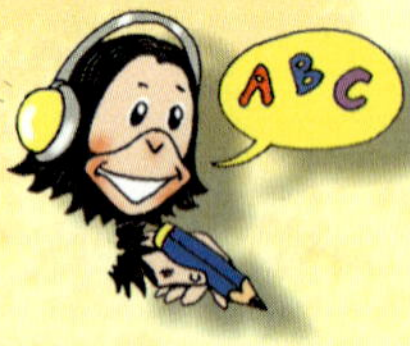

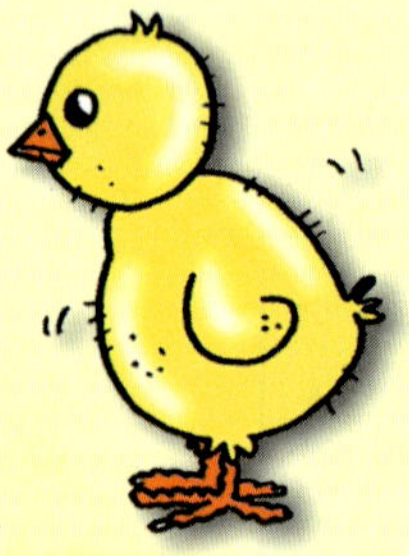

chick

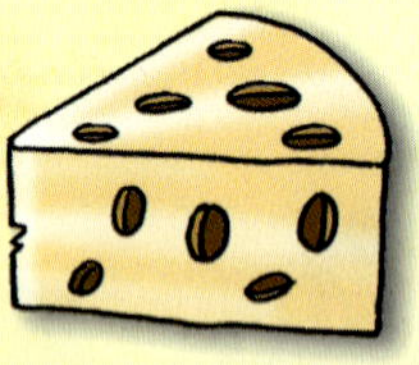

cheese

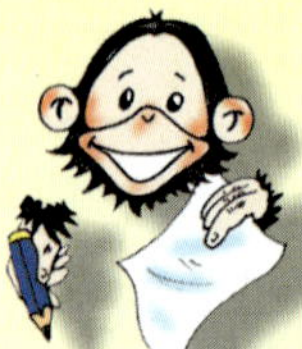

a, e, i, o or u?

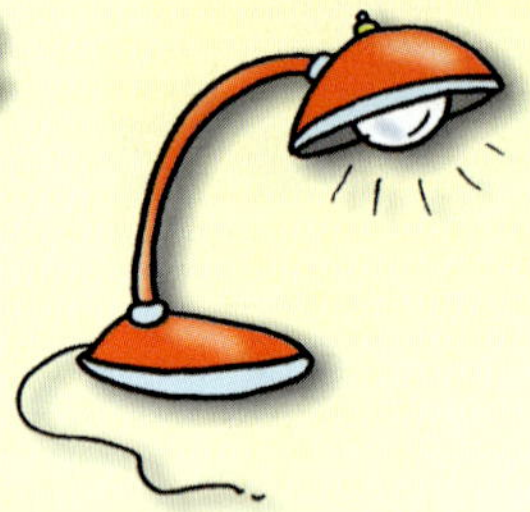

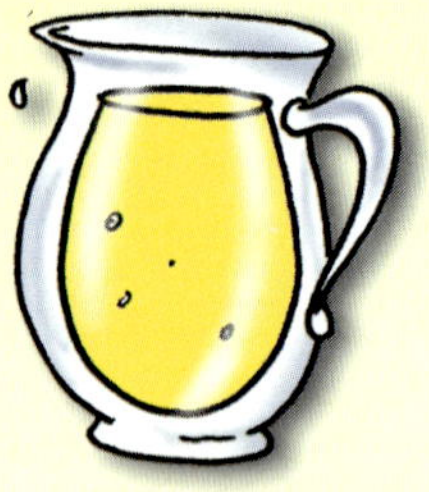

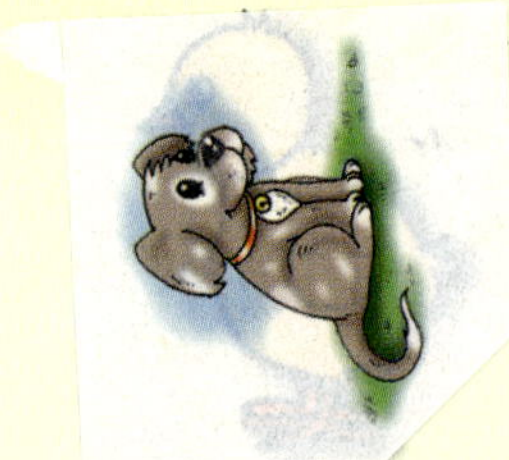

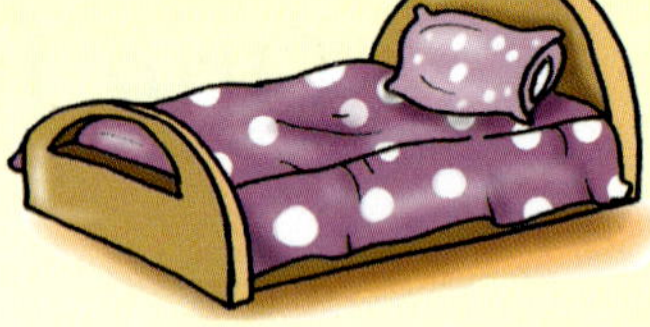

l_a_mp   j __ g   ch __ ck   b __ d

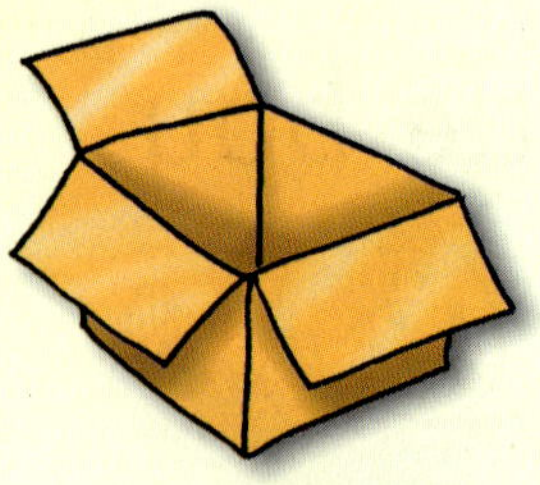

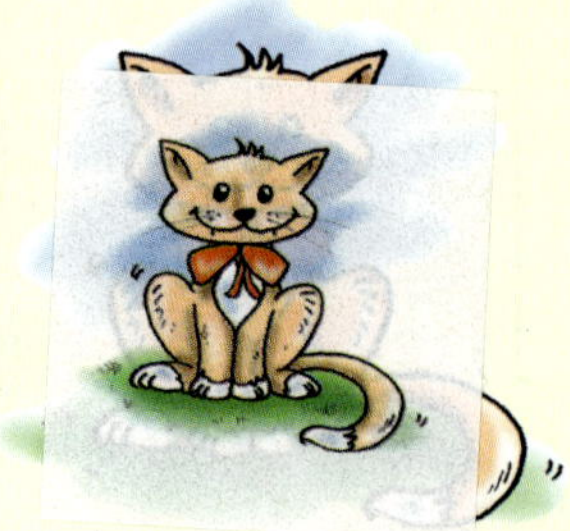

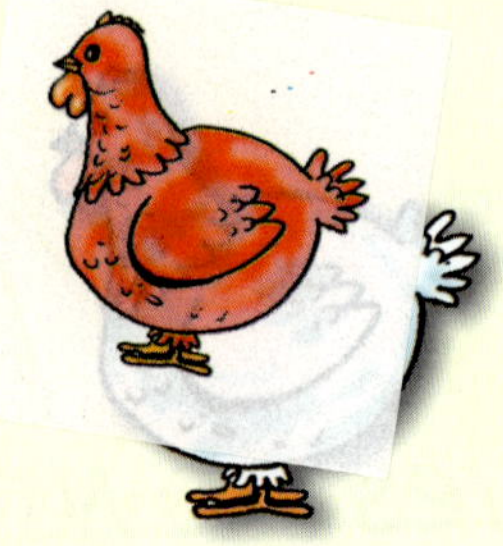

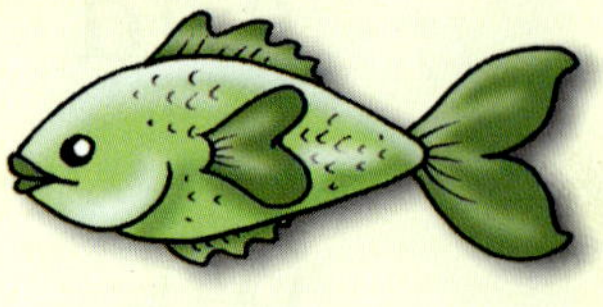

b __ x   c __ t   h __ n   f __ sh

5 10

1

tea

BRAVO! Bravo!
Thumbs up!

Full marks! GENIUS! Number 1! PERFECT!

Excellent! Right on!

TIP TOP! Right on! SUPER!

chick, cheese

Chick, chick, chick, chick, chicken,

Lay a little egg for me!

Chick, _ _ _ _ _, ☐ chick, chick, chicken,

I want one for my tea!

I haven't had an egg since Sunday,

And now it's half past three!

So, chick, chick, chick, chick, chicken,

Lay a little egg for me!

thumb, thimble

th th

thumb

thimble

the, this

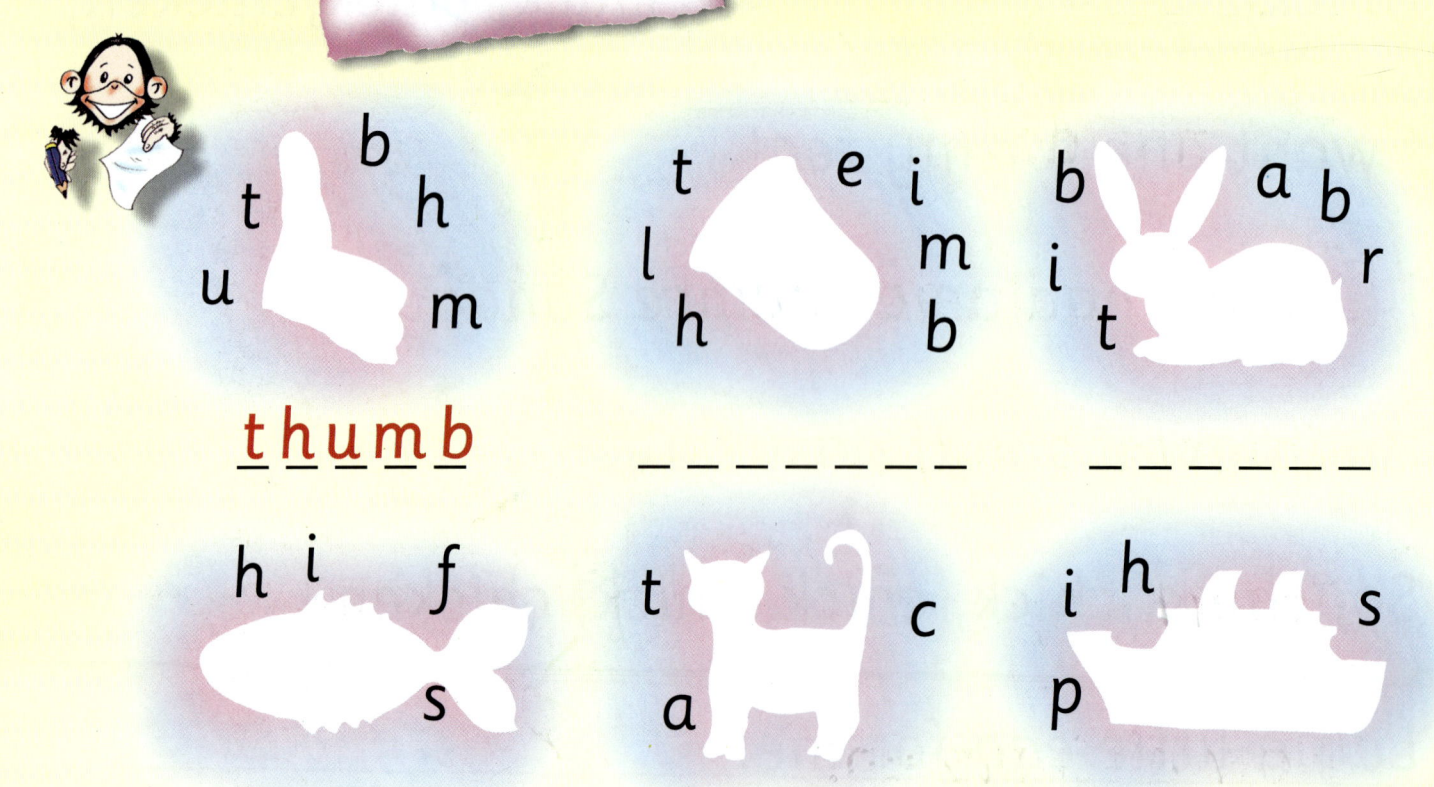

thumb

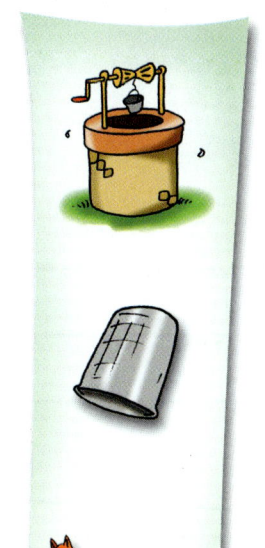

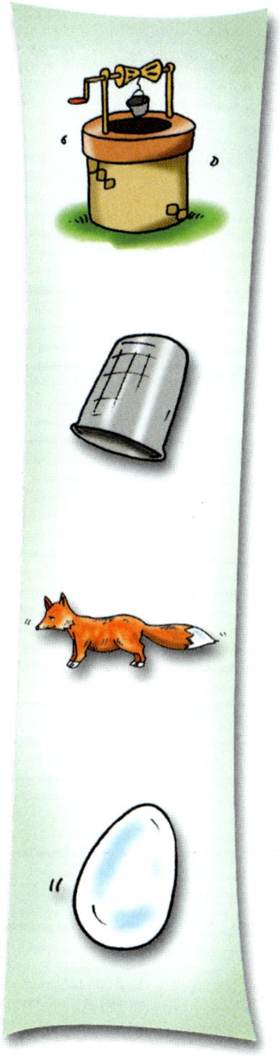

thumb, thimble

bed   bell   (well)

thimble   thumb   tree

frog   fox   box

egg   jug   mug

_ _ _ _ _ s [ ] up,

Thumbs down,

Turn round and round!

Thumbs down,

Thumbs up,

Now all jump up!

35

photo, dolphin

ph ph

photo

dolphin

f or ph?

fish   ele_ _ant   dol_ _in   _ox

photo, dolphin

ch ph sh th

_t h_umb   _ _ick   _ _oto   _ _eep

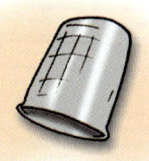

_ _eese   dol_ _in   _ _ip   _ _imble

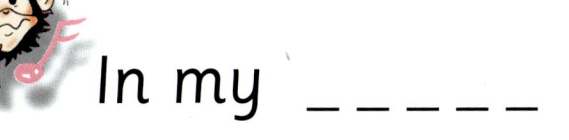

In my _ _ _ _ _ _

You can see

A little _ _ _ _ _ _ _ _

In the sea!

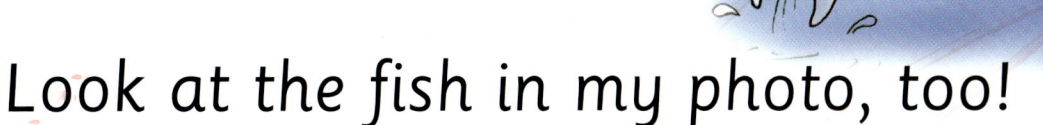

Look at the fish in my photo, too!

The fish is green,

And the sea is blue!

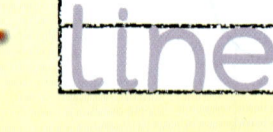

Rhyme Time 1

cake

snake

pine

line

mole

hole

cat/**snake** pine/king dog/mole

lamp/line flag/cake hole/fox

Rhyme Time 1

a pine on the _line_

a snake on the ____

a mole in the ____

Pat - a - cake, pat - a - cake, baker's man,

Bake me a ____ ☐ as fast as you can!

Roll it and pat it, and mark it with T,

And put it in the oven for Tommy and me!

Rhyme Time II

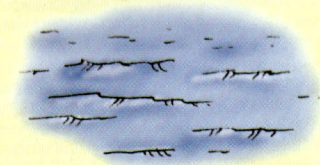

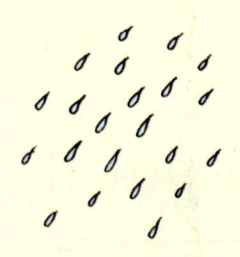

sea

tea

rain

train

s <u>e a</u>   tr _ _ n   r _ _ n   t _ _

Rhyme Time 11

seateatrainraindolphinphoto

I saw a ship a-sail,

A-sail on the ___,

And oh, but it was full

Of lovely things for ___!

Rhyme Time III

boat

coat

goat

three ✓

two ✗

five ✗

eight ✗   seven ✗

nine ✗   one ✓

Rhyme Time III

b o a t — sea

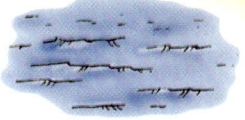

h _ le — train

t _ _ — cake

sn _ ke — mole

r _ _ n → goat

Put on your hat,

Put on your coat,

For we have a journey

Away on a boat!

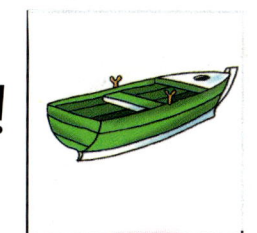

Big and small!

a A	A
b B	B
c C	C
d D	D
e E	E
f F	F
g G	G
h H	H
i I	I
j J	J
k K	K
l L	L
m M	M

Big and small!

ABCDEFGHIJKLM,

I can sing the alphabet,

Can you do the same?

Big and small!

n N	N
o O	O
p P	P
q Q	Q
r R	R
s S	S
t T	T
u U	U
v V	V
w W	W
x X	X
y Y	Y
z Z	Z

Big and small!

cat
lamp
horse
pin
jug
rabbit
orange
window

c a t
C A T

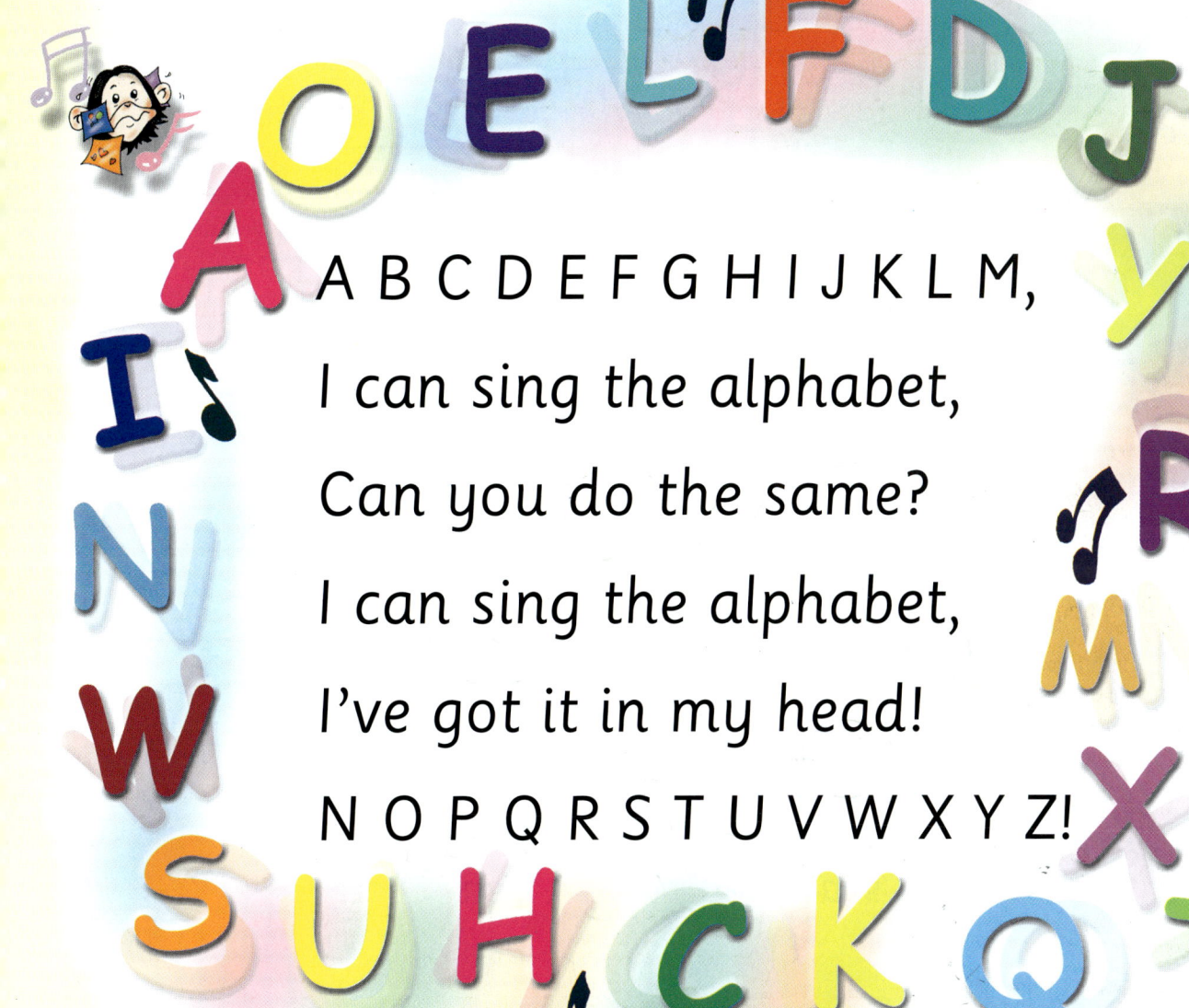

A B C D E F G H I J K L M,
I can sing the alphabet,
Can you do the same?
I can sing the alphabet,
I've got it in my head!
N O P Q R S T U V W X Y Z!

Now I know!

rabbit   snake

sheep   mouse

cat   kangaroo

pony   hen

fox (box) fox   fox   fox

mug   mug (jug) mug   mug

coat   coat   coat (goat) coat

well   bell   bell   bell   bell

sea   sea (tea) sea   sea

Now I know!

Star light, _ _ _ _ ☐ bright,

First star I see tonight,

I wish I may, I wish I might,

Have the wish I wish tonight!

Picture Word Cards

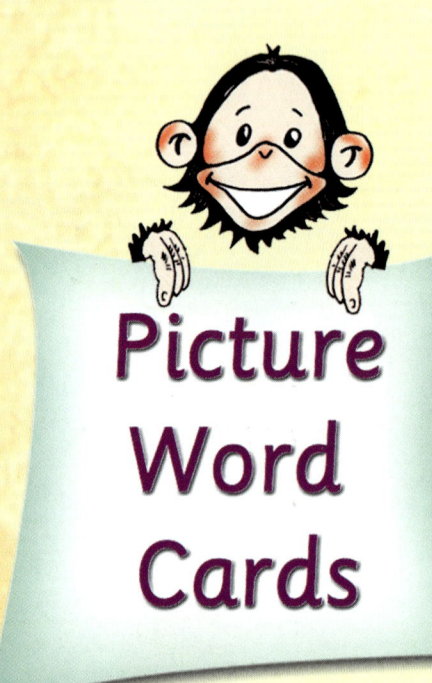

51

dog	cat
egg	hen
bell	hat
vest	well

53

box	fox
jug	zip
jam	mug
pony	yoyo

55

queen	star
sheep	king
ship	fish
cheese	chick

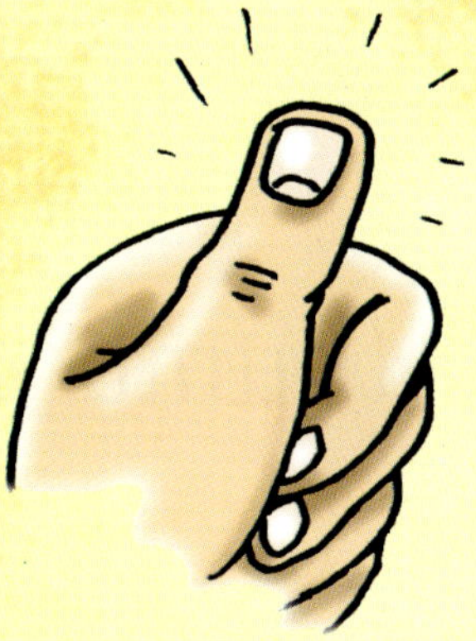

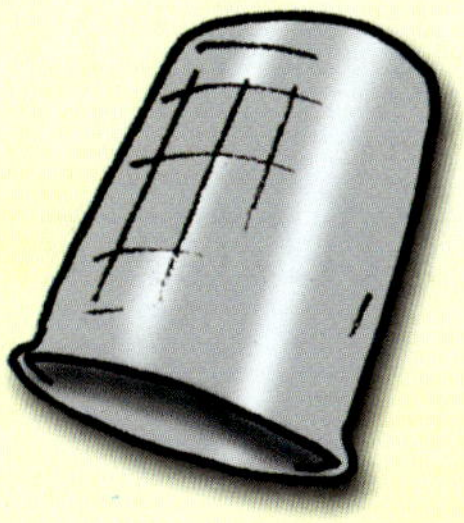

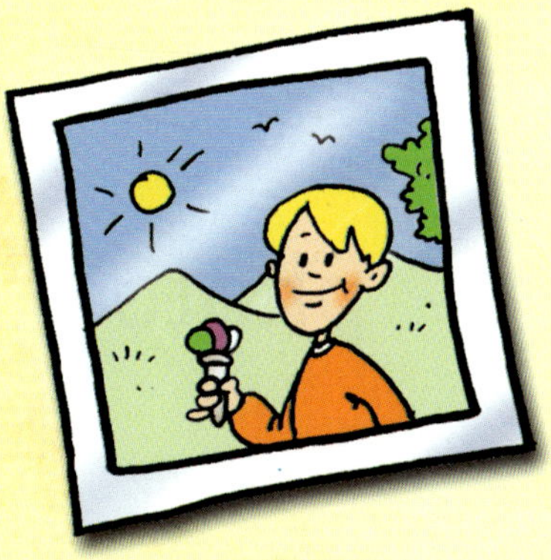

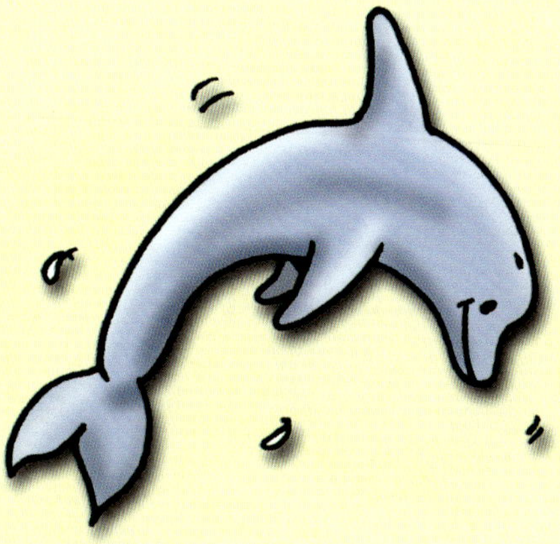

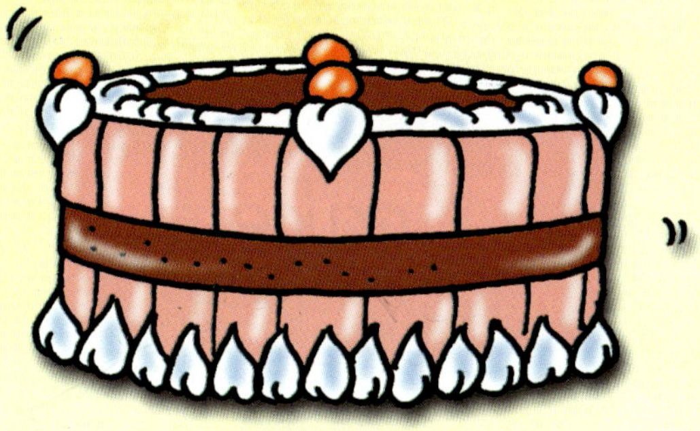

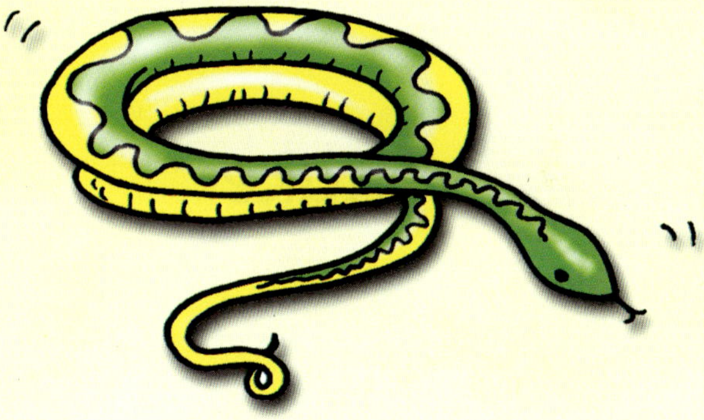

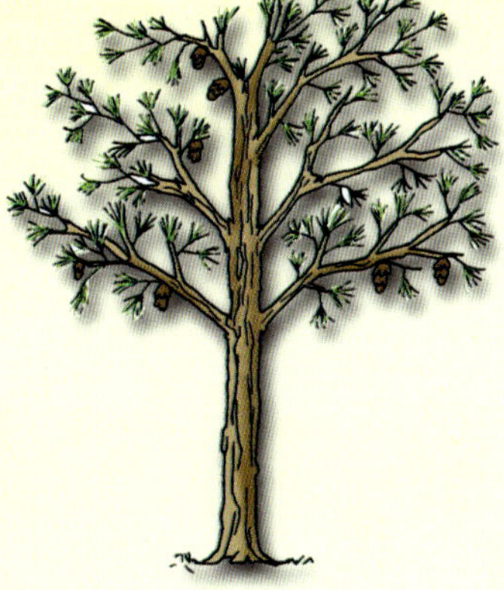

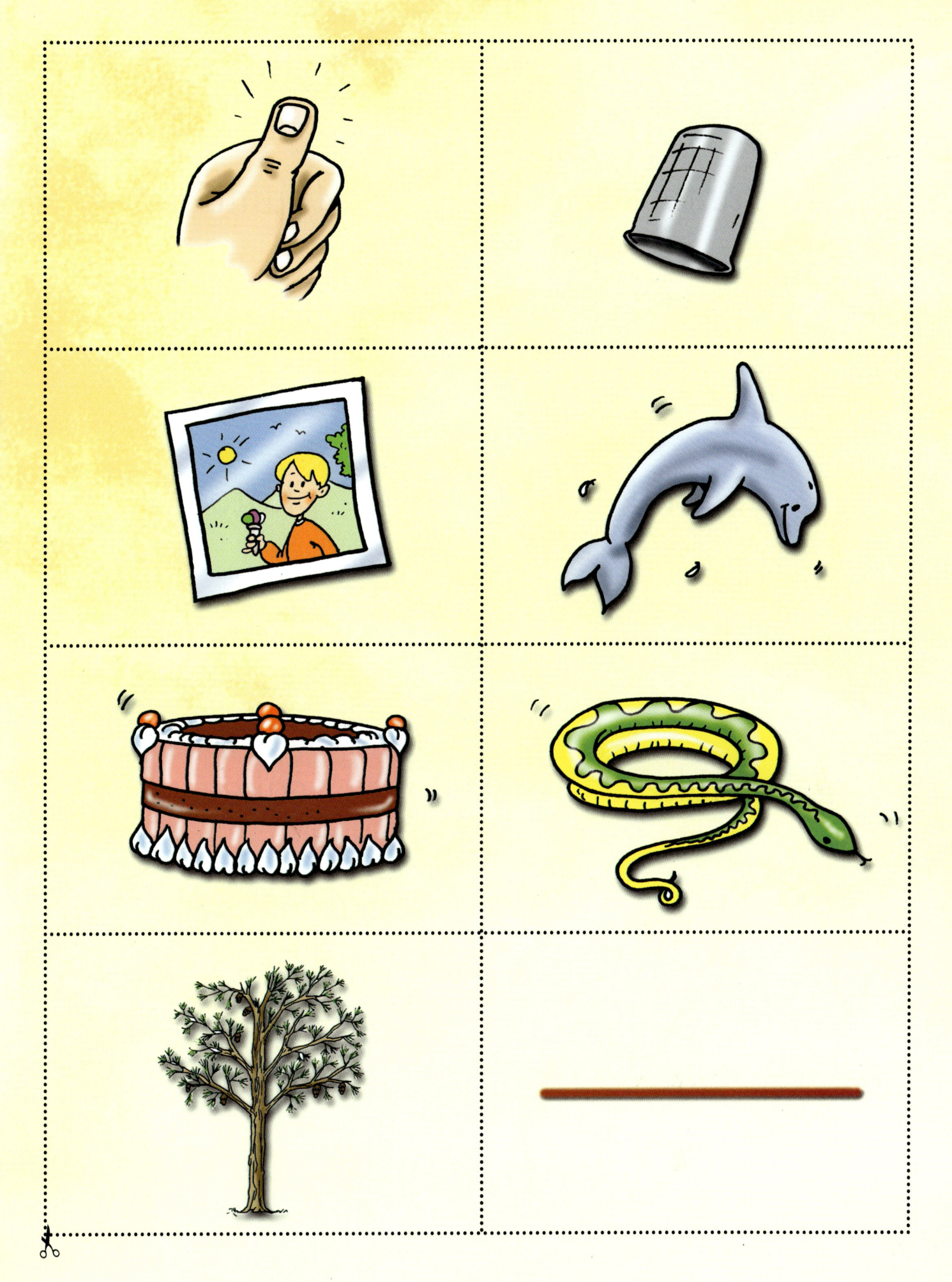

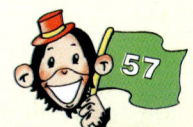

thimble	thumb
dolphin	photo
snake	cake
line	pine

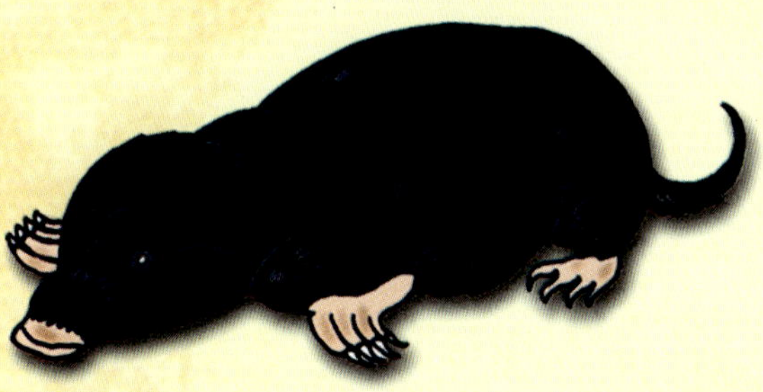

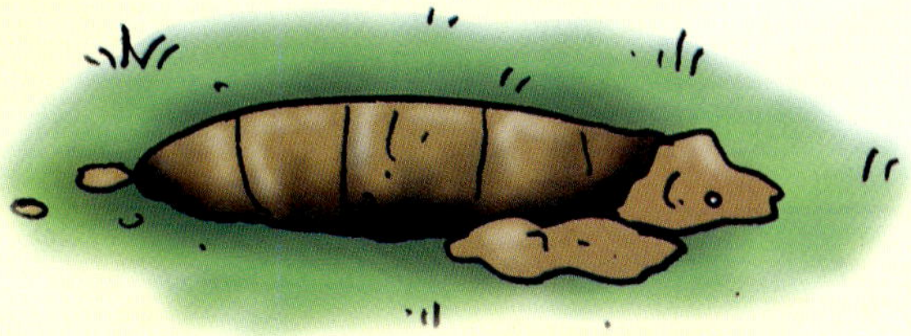

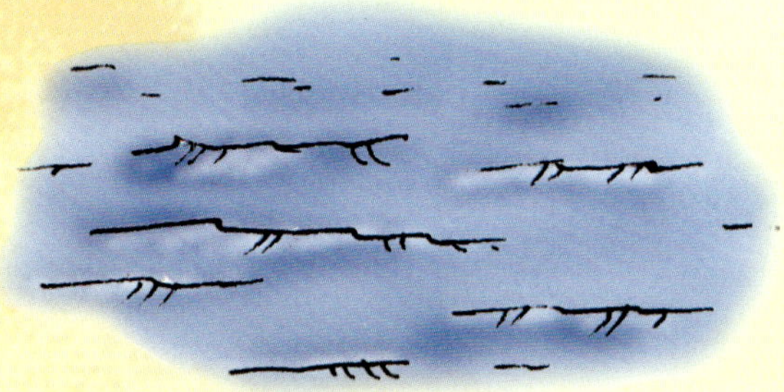

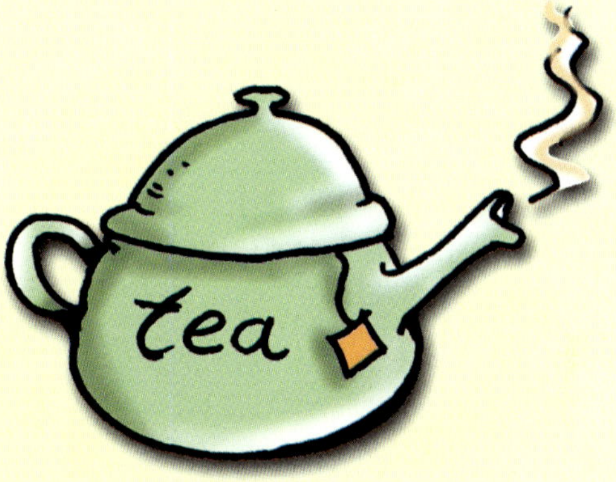
tea

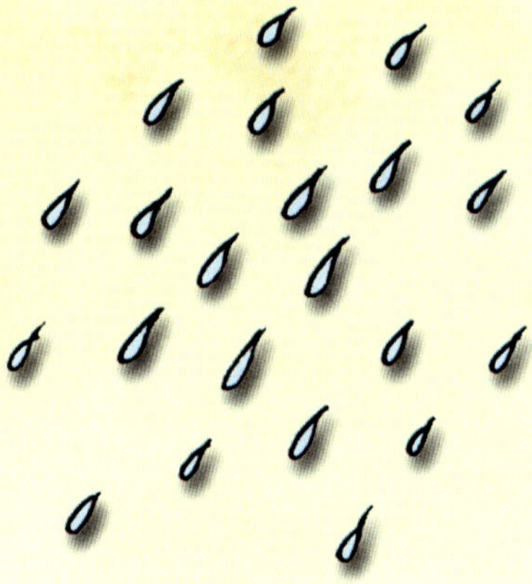

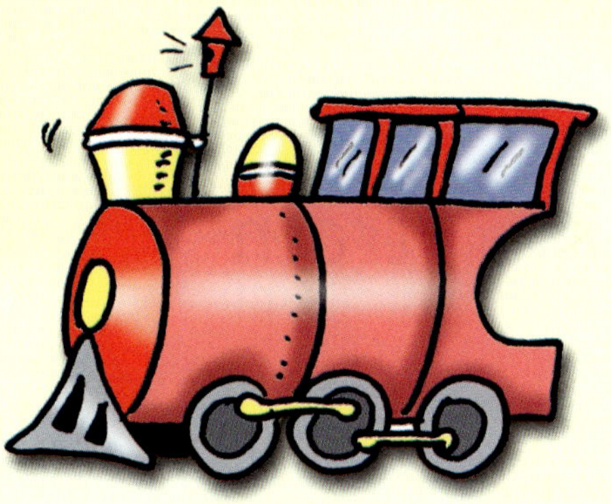

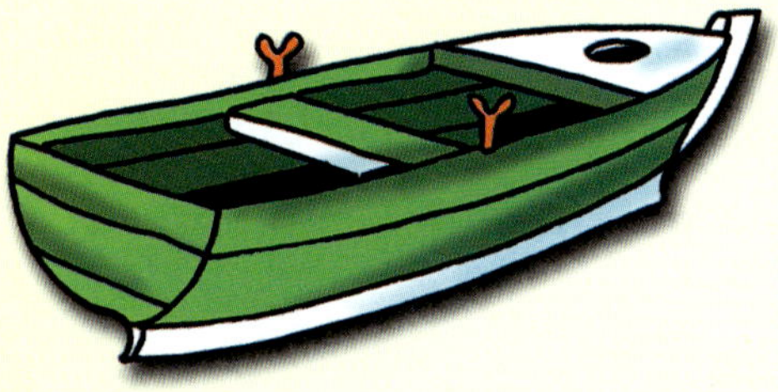

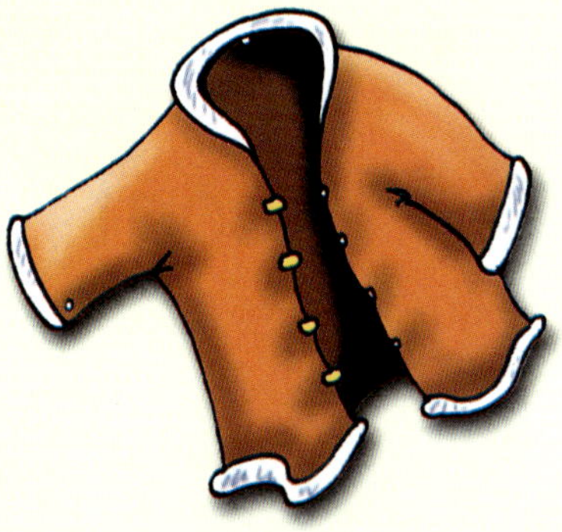

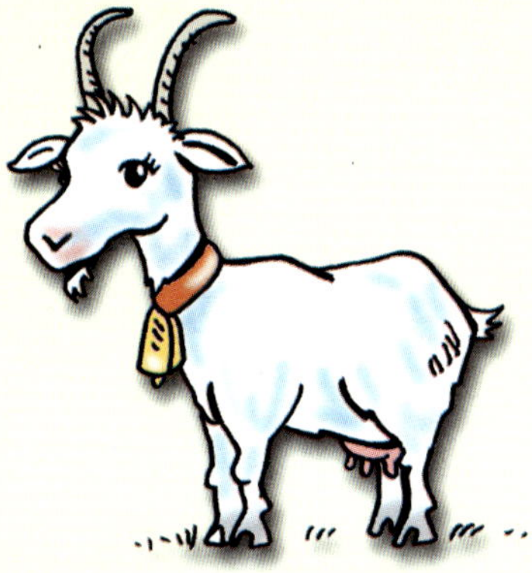

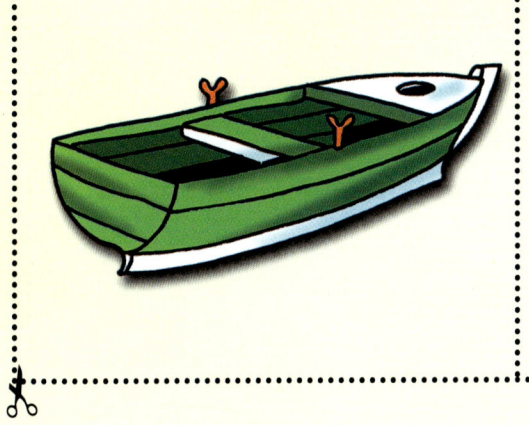

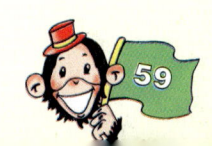

hole	mole
tea	sea
train	rain

goat	coat	boat

🔴	🟡
🔵	🟢
1	2
3	4
5	6
7	8
9	10

yellow	red
green	blue
two	one
four	three
six	five
eight	seven
ten	nine

Letterfun

Alphabet Award!

To: Assad

Well done!